Ian Hibburt
And the Moon still shines
And other poems

Book 3

First published by Busybird Publishing 2021

Copyright © 2021 Ian Hibburt

ISBN
978-1-922691-04-0

This book is copyright. Apart from any fair dealing for the purposes of study, research, criticism, review, or as otherwise permitted under the Copyright Act, no part may be reproduced by any process without written permission. Enquiries should be made through the publisher.

This is a work of fiction. Any similarities between places and characters are a coincidence.

Cover Image and design: Pexels (Johannes Plenio), Busybird Publishing

Layout and typesetting: Busybird Publishing

Busybird Publishing
2/118 Para Road
Montmorency, Victoria
Australia 3094

www.busybird.com.au

*I dedicate this book to all my special friends
And to Dianne, my soul-mate and inspiration.
Also the others who have helped.*

*Special thanks to Margaret, Sarah and Mary
For all their encouragement and understanding.*

Other books by Ian Hibburt
Angels Weep
Pathways

Contents

Chapter 1
HOPE — 1

And the Moon still shines	2
Better Days Ahead	4
Dreams on hold	6
Future Dreams	8
Hindsight is 20/20	9
It's Time	10
Nothing moves	12
Through The Fire	14
In The Darkness	15
HOPE	16

Chapter 2
BLUES — 17

Black Dog	18
Black	19
Like a Stone	20
Lockdown Blues	21
Thoughts on moving on	24
I Have The Right	25
No one is There	26
Lost Dreams	27
Seeking the Good	29
Progress?	30

Chapter 3
MUSINGS — 31

Quiescence	32
Days of Innocence	34
Conversations of the Heart	35
Echoes	36
Eleven nine twentytwenty	37
Desire and achievement	40
All is Quiet	42
The Room of Secrets	44
What's left?	45
Night Dreamers	49
Renovation of my soul	50
Thoughts of a Monk	52
In Between	54

Chapter 4
LOVE
57

A Rose in a Cemetery	58
She Cries	59
Love Saved Me	60
Our Love	61
Sleep My Angel	62
Last flight to Venus	63
Our Bridge	64
I Love You When ...	65
Precious Thing	66
May the Angels	67

Chapter 5
GREEN NATURE
69

My Day has Begun	70
Mid Winter	71
Morning	72
Mountain Brumbies	73
The Tides	74
Stars are shining	75
The Crows	76
Reflections on a River	78
Southern Ocean	79
The Beach on the Edge of the World	80
Pukekura Park	81
Family Beach Time	82
The Pelicans Have Gone	83
The Forest Chapel	84

Chapter 6
TRUTH & CHANGE
85

A tear silently falls	86
Truth	88
Gates of Paradise	90
The New Normal	93
The Halls of Knowledge?	94
The beauty of Healing	96
Small Lives	98
Says the Brown Owl	100
White Eagle Returns	102
The Elephant Again	103
Second Destiny	105
Night Steed	106

Chapter 1
HOPE

Ian Hibburt

And the Moon still shines

High above the trees the Moon is shining
It's silver light, gleams on the leaves
The evening breeze sighing in the branches

The Moon has seen it all, through the seasons
Through the ages, eons of peace,
Then the ascent of Man.
Born with the finger-print of the creator
In his soul and a talent for good and evil
What will He choose?
A tragedy, to destroy the Good with the Bad
But, it always has been thus:-
The innocent suffer for the guilty
Is there no justice in this world?
Apparently not.
And Man the architect of His own
Destruction!

And the eternal Moon will watch from on high
Unmoved by the plight of Man
And what of the innocents?
Are there no Angels of mercy to help?
Will God watch his children playing with fire
Even after he warned them not to?
Leave them to learn their own lessons?
The answers to these questions are hard
To understand.

All I know is, disruption is here
Everything is being turned upside down
And we must seek help from above
If we are to survive

Look up at the Moon
It will rise in the east tomorrow
A constant in this world of change
The silver Moon shines on.

Better Days Ahead

Good days to be a Pessimist,
So much bad news to work with
So many things to be angry about.
But I'm not going down that road
As easy as it seems to give in
To the negative.

Better days to be an optimist
To see the opportunities hiding in the shadows
Just waiting for the sun to shine.
And bring them to light.
So many acts of kindness I have seen.
Strangers, talking to each other
Without fear, are now brothers and sisters
In this fight against the unknown.
We are guided to consider
What really matters in this life.

Many of us are off the endless treadmill
Of earning more, spending more,
And crave a simpler life where
The pace is slow.
And time is measured by the seasons
Not by the seconds.
Yes we all need time to breathe
To get in touch with our
Spiritual selves.
And we do not go on forever,
As we all know.
Our life here, is learning
For eternity
Which is only a heartbeat away.

Dreams on hold

They called it lockdown,
It should be called lock-up
Or did they think that sounded too harsh
Too close to the truth.
But it's only for our own good,
For your health and well-being
We must lock you down.
We are all in this together
And the carefully doctored figures
Tell the grim truth, No, "story"
"Do not dream this will be over anytime soon,
No, it's worse than we thought."
In this age of misinformation
The first casualty is the truth,
To seek unbiased facts is like
Chasing a mirage

And now the second casualty
Is our freedom
What is next?
Well, thankfully, this will soon to be over
And we will all have been given
A huge wake-up call
How easily it was done,
How quickly our rights were dissolved
"To save us all from this threat."
No, when this is over we will discover,
What really went down
And how close we came to losing it all.
We must learn from this.
We have been saved by forces
Greater than us.

Future Dreams

The unborn future awaits its time
To be formed into existence
Our dreams need to be given space
And energy to grow
Protected from those negative thoughts
Which would destroy them.

It's all about possibilities, vision
And the creative spark
That will ignite the flame of desire
To bring that new thing into existence

I'm believing in the dream
Tomorrow the sun will shine
And love will be reborn
Breathing life into my languishing dreams
Empowering – creating a new reality
In which they can exist.

Hindsight is 20/20

Time gives us perspective
Looking back –
Of course we didn't know
It would end like this.
Some things were right,
Some things were wrong
Some things we need
To forgive others for,
Some things we need
To forgive ourselves for –
And move on
Never go back
The future awaits.

It's Time

A gentle melody weaves its way
Through my memories,
Dragging the past behind it.
Refugees from the past
With memories that refuse to die.
Good times, bad times.
Regrets of the heart
The hurt that won't heal
Battle scars of Love –
That went bad.
A sadness that haunts my mind,
Questions, which have no answers.

How long must this go on?
When will it be time
To let it all go?
Time to draw a line under
All these memories
And say "I did the best I could"
And leave it at that,
Forgive myself
And let myself heal.
I have the power to forgive
To allow the past sink into
The sea of forgetfulness
And finally close the door
On the past forever
And walk away, free.

Living for today
Looking for the dream
That's coming true for me.

Nothing moves

Nothing moves
All is quiet
No Joy to greet me
In the morning.

We are in lock-down.
Wearing masks to keep us safe
This bug can kill us;
But so can isolation, loneliness
And depression.

In the war of the worlds,
The bug killed the aliens
And we all cheered
Now the bug is killing us
And nobody is cheering.

It's not like this is new,
It's only new for our generation.
We thought science had all the answers
And took them for granted;
Left them to tinker with
Pharmaceutical recipes
To "manage" our diseases.

Just like our health,
Give me some medication
And a handful of vitamins
And I'll be on my way
More money to be made today.

How long did we really think
The good times would last?
The endless chase for
Fortune and fame
Has ended.

Ian Hibburt

Through The Fire

We all must walk through the Fire
To be reborn, after we have been tested
By the flames.

Burn the dross of our past
Till it is no more
Forgive those we have to and
Let the past, be the past
And forgotten.
Dead and buried
Cleansed by fire
Purified in the crucible of truth

And when it is all over
See what remains –
Refined Gold
Life reborn
Without the pattern of
Sin and failure
Joy is reborn
Love is abundant
Happiness abounds
Surly this is Paradise found.

In The Darkness

In the darkness
The tiniest spark of hope
Is born.

A tiny speck of crystal light
A star in the vast darkness.

So from within the dark
And endless night,
Hope shines and grows
Until eventually
We are bathed in the
Brilliance of its light!

Ian Hibburt

HOPE

Live with hope in your Heart
Leave room in your soul for believing
And one day
Heaven and Earth
Will be in harmony
Then the impossible
Will happen for you
Opportunities will appear
Where you thought there were none
So live with Hope in your Heart.

Chapter 2
BLUES

Black Dog

Out walking I met a Black Dog on my way
He seemed friendly so we continued
Down paths that he knew.
Darker and lonelier, into dark valleys
Until we overlooked ... the abyss
Never-ending, drawing us in.
I stared into the abyss
"Give up Hope, Drop in and Die"
It called.
Compelled and transfixed I wavered
On that precipice ...
Then I heard a cry
"You are needed here!"
Jolted from my trance
I'll not throw everything away,
Just because I'm having a Bad Day!

"Get away you evil dog"
I have a life to live
And things to do

Black

The darkness which hides
Those forgotten corners
Of my mind,
The darkness which grows
And encroaches when
I'm feeling down.
What is this Yin to my Yang?
Negative to my positive?
What is this darkness hiding in the
Forgotten corners of my mind?
Waiting for its opportunity to
Overwhelm me and drag my soul
Down into despondency.
It has no power but that which I give it.
Black has a place in the order of things –
Part, but not all.

Any artist will tell you there are many blacks
Any artist will know that colours are brighter
When set against a background of black.
So what about Black?
A very good servant,
But a very bad master!

Black has its place in the
Order of things – part
But not the whole.

Like a Stone

The pain of losing you is unavoidable
Goodbyes, sad eyes,
Grasping the thorn and the rose
Into the deep end
In sorrows tight embrace
I am drowning
Deeper and deeper
Like a stone
Falling ... falling ...
Then bump
I hit the bottom ...
Silence,
Silence.
Slowly the pain ebbs away
And light fills my soul
And I am rising ...
Faster and faster
Returning to the surface
And the light.
Joy floods my soul.

Lockdown Blues

I am lost.
No direction
Dreams have all flown
Becalmed.
A yacht without wind.

And now the reality bites!
We have no choice
Our freedom has been taken
Confined by rules
Enforced by Police
Punished with fines

I've been positive,
This will soon be over
This will not get me down.

Then it all changes again
And hope is crushed
Like a snail on concrete
And I am falling into
The abyss of despair

Ian Hibburt

But, wait, before I give up –
I've been here before –
And what did I do?

Yes, I remember the thought –
You are needed to help others –
To be part of the solution.
Don't give in
Ask your friends for help.

So I asked my friends for help
And help was given.

I've got this all wrong
I've been looking
At what I can't do –
When all the time there is,
What I still can do.

My dreams can motivate me,
To plan and prepare so I am ready to go
When we are set free.

My imagination has no chains
It can fly!

Poetry can be written
Pictures painted
Books read
Lessons finished
Diplomas achieved
Houses painted
Stuff organised
Body exercised
And trained
Love given
And received
Yes, I have more than I thought

Thoughts on moving on

Sometimes you choose your path
And then quietly move in that direction
Then after a while you talk with an old friend
And realise with a little jolt –
We have moved apart
And we are experiencing
Life differently

Sometimes the challenges come thick and fast
Forcing you to seek the strength within
To get you through.
We choose our path
And we must see it through
Sacrifices will be required
And rewards will be won.

I Have The Right

I have the right to protect myself
I have the right to my personal space
I do not have to give to everyone
Who wants to take.
I work hard to be positive, at peace
And full of joy and energy
This is mine, not yours.
If I choose to give you some –
That's okay, – my choice
But you must not steal my Energy,
For yourself!
So I'm placing a shield of blue energy
Around my life, protecting me
And keeping me safe.
Angels are kind and loving,
But, don't think
You can take advantage of them.
They are more than capable
Of protecting themselves.

Ian Hibburt

No one is There

Into the ever darkening forest I walked
Further into the gloom
Down, down into the valley of despair
Carrying feelings of hurt and failure
Down among the darkness and silence
Down among the dead things –
I am angry at myself,
Putting myself down
For not achieving the impossible goal.
Feelings of sadness and loss,
That hollow feeling in my soul

There is no hope.
No light at the end of the tunnel
I am alone.
Nobody else here.

So this is it –
Am I going to stay here?
Feeling sad and alone?
I look up and see a stairway
I choose to leave this place
Turning my back on those bad memories –
I begin to climb out, one step at a time
Up the stairway
Into the light

Lost Dreams

Down into the dark forest
The path winds its way
Wandering deeper and deeper
Into the gloom.
What am I seeking here
In the dark side of my soul?
Deep emotions of pain and loneliness
Are waiting to be heard
So this is a reliquary
Of lost dreams
Still-born and doomed to die.
I'm here to mourn
What might have been
What a sad place
Darkness and depression
Why do I hold on to

This evidence of failure?
Perhaps it's time –
I've acknowledged the pain
I've heard your voice
And now it's time to for you to go
I light a candle in this
Basement of lost dreams
Light fills the room
And my mind clears
The hurt is gone
And so are the lost dreams
All that energy tied up
In grief and loss
Is now set free
The heaviness of my soul is lifting
And the sparkling light of hope
Fills my soul.

Seeking the Good

We are seeking the good –
The good things in life we are given
Looking past the drama
And negative fears
That storm our minds,
Seeking to steal our peace.

Seeking the good things
Hiding among the troubles
Which surround us.
And finding those gems
Of goodness and light.
We are lifted by Joy
And begin to feel
The awe of creation.
Energy floods our soul
Empowering us to fly
Above the troubles
Into the sky of God's Love
We may never return!

Progress?

We have always had Faith
And also the early settlers who
Came seeking a better life.

And where are we now?
Have we lost our way?
Lost our values?

And where is the family farm?
Now it is just acreage
Tended by computer-driven tractors
Growing crops for overseas companies.

I'm not a Luddite; but not all
Progress is for the better.

Chapter 3
MUSINGS

Quiescence

Neither happy or sad:
Just being; letting it all
Roll over me –

I am caught in a back-water
Away from the main flow of life.

Time to let those shadows materialise
And express themselves.
This is healthy –
Part of me yearns for
The security of my old life,
But, that was only an illusion –
Dining at the Captain's table
On the Titanic.
Remember the guilt,
Fear and condemnation of the old life
You are free!

Deal with these memories
Which refuse to die.
View your Past with Love,
Compassion and Mercy.

Yes, I did this and I did that
Made this decision and that decision,
Kept the peace, made do,
Tolerated frustration.
But, hey, what's done is done.
Time to draw a LINE under it
And move on.

Moving on!

Days of Innocence

When we had laughter and fun in the sun
Running free,
Without rules and punishment.
Those were days of innocence
When our dreams had wings to fly
And emotions were free to flow.
Before we were tamed into subjection
And just like that our inner light
Was snuffed out.
And we were left wondering
What did we do wrong?
Where did our Joy go?

And years later, if we are lucky,
We can return to the age of innocence
And bring Healing to our younger selves.
Nothing is as it seems,
Reality changes as we do.

Conversations of the Heart

When did it all start?
As a child I believed in God –
A sense of wonder;
Standing in the morning sun
Looking at the nasturtiums
Growing among the rocks and thinking
The innocent question,
Who made all of this?
"I did, I made all this I am God
The creator" he said.
I still remember that first time
My spirit reached out to God
And the conversation of the Heart
We had.

Ian Hibburt

Echoes

Echoes of memories
Drift by, briefly igniting
Feelings of loss and regret
And my soul resonates
To their bitter/sweet pain
Love, Lost and found.
And passion that never grew enough
To take root in my heart
Shadows crossing my mind
And the fleeting pulse
Of memories of emotions
Long forgotten –
The life I lived and
The life I might have lived –
And now the day,
It is new, and what will we do?
Listen to the voices of the past?
Or just let it all go
And open your heart –
To a new Love.

Eleven nine twentytwenty

Deep in the catacombs under the city
Hidden from sight are the secret places
Where Christians came to worship
Signs of their faith graffiti the walls
Illuminated by their lamps.

Sixty years ago in Romania
Religion and Faith was banned
By the communist government
Churches were closed
People were not allowed
To hold meetings
And your neighbours would
Spy on you.
Penalties were severe large fines –
And if you were poor, imprisonment.

It's to save our health we are told
We must control your every move
And don't put your thoughts on social media
Because if they don't like them – the police
Will visit your house and arrest you!
Truth is the first victim of this virus –
The news is now poisoned with lies and half truths

Ian Hibburt

Freedom is the second victim of this virus –
The diggers fought for our freedom
From oppression, now it is lost.

Faith is the third victim of this virus
We are being bombarded with visions of fear,
Painted in sickly negative colours on our screens
The end point for this
Is continually being put on hold,
People are giving up Hope,
Livelihoods are lost,
Businesses closed ,
Never to open again.

And what of our Faith that sustained us
In good times and bad?
Religious services are prohibited
Weddings not allowed
Funerals, no mourners allowed
Five people only.
We cannot join for worship
We cannot pray together
We have no fellowship

So we do what they did in ancient Rome
Keep our faith secret
And pray in private.

And like the Romanian Christians
We will suffer and plant the seeds of faith
Which will grow in better times

We will pray direct to God on our own
And God will hear us and show us
A way through this –
When this is over
Things must change
And we will never take our
Freedom, Truth and Faith for granted.

Desire and achievement

The endless pure blue sky
Taunts me with the desire to fly
To leave this earth of pain
Fly away, never return again.
But, within the cold dirt of earth –
Gold is to be found.
And being part of the community of Man
Joy and love are found.
Man is a dysfunctional being.
Brilliant and stupid at the same time!
Capable of many extremes.
Put on earth to figure it out
That's what this life is all about.

We have the choice
Ephemeral dreams come and go
Potentialities in space and time
Waiting to be called into existence

We have the power to bring them to life
Also the responsibility to finish the process
Once we have begun.

Lives are littered with half-finished dreams
Projects started with enthusiasm
Only to die from lack of resolve.

So we have the choice –
To start, continue and finish our dreams.
Giving up is not an option anymore.
Face our fears
Stare them down
And strike that first blow
And continue until
It is done and we have
Won our goal.

All is Quiet

All is quiet
I am sitting – quietly
The critics in my head
Have stopped talking
They have gotten bored
With being ignored
And have moved out.

And the Narc has gone too ...
Its cover has been blown
Its ability to coerce
And manipulate has gone
Evaporated, like when the Sun hits
The early morning dew.

And my Internal Saboteur
Has told me it's not fun anymore
Now that he can no longer hide from sight
And his ruse is blown every time

No! They have all moved out
And I feel so good!
No nagging worry about unfinished business
No disquiet in my soul
Just Peace and Love.
No one querying every decision
No fear, No guilt, No sorrow.

My life has changed in every way
I'm not leaking energy.
Now I'm living the life
I am supposed to live.
Love, Freedom, Joy.
21/1/21.

The Room of Secrets

I'm opening the door,
To the room of secrets
All those thoughts and feelings
I fought so hard to deny
Time to reclaim the
Fallow lands of forbidden life
I'm acknowledging I want
A full and interesting life
I'm owning my life
The good and the bad
And everything in between.
I'm opening the door
And now there are
No more secrets to hide.
No more guilt and pain
Though I still bear the scars
Of too much self-denial
Too much loss
Regret traces its tears
Across my soul
And it is finished.

What's left?

After the great disruption
When everything is thrown up in the air,
And in a moment of extreme clarity
I see everything as it really is –
With a flash of knowing
That I have been tricked
I am repulsed at the lies
I have been told.

Now I want to destroy it all.
Walk away from all of this deceit.
Walk away from the endless search
For Peace and Happiness
Walk away from the mirage of their truth
Walk away from believing that this should work
If only I have enough faith,
If only I am humble enough,
Keep trying keep chasing
The next revelation
That will answer all my questions!

No! No! not any more
This stops now!
This is not the truth!
This is an endless litany of lies,
An endless search, an endless quest,
A Sunday fix that only lasts until Wednesday
Keep believing and when I die
I will go to heaven.

Now that I have walked away,
Now that I've given away the rules
And laws and beliefs to start over
I've woken from an endless dream.
"Hello God, it's Ian here."
"Hello Ian, I've been waiting
For you to awake,"
Look at this – the simple truth
The truth is simple
Isn't it.
WOW.

Eternity and all its glory
Is just over there –
But this is not just some head-trip
Not some pleasant spiritual day dream
No, this is real on every level
The spiritually awake person
Still needs to attend to practical things
Such as work and payment
Planting and harvesting,
Weeds still grow in the garden
Of the enlightened one
And he still needs to pull them out
Feet in the earth.

So what's left?
I thought it is all bad,
Nothing of value,
Just needs to be burnt, destroyed.
And so it should be
But within the dross there is
A kernel of gold that survives the crucible
Of the refining fire.
So the lies and half-truths
Are burnt away and what is pure
Survives.

Ian Hibburt

This is what is left,
The pure heart that seeks
And gives LOVE.
The pure heart that seeks
TRUTH and rejects lies.
The pure heart that GIVES
Without counting the cost,
Without expectation of repayment.
The pure heart that finds JOY
In the simplest things.
The pure heart that finds BEAUTY
And treasures it.

So it wasn't all bad,
I've walked away with these
Five pure gold nuggets.
If we keep the pure essence
Of our experiences good and bad
Then nothing has been in vane
Only the dross has been lost
And that's not a bad thing.
So what's left?
Five nuggets of pure GOLD.
That's what's left.

Night Dreamers

And the people of the world
Are dreaming tonight –
Asleep in their beds.
Some of us are awake listening to
The voices in the night
Telling us what they know and feel.

And for a while Heaven and earth inter-weave
The divine road opens for us to travel
To worlds out there –
And I will tread the pathways among the stars
Through the velvet night
Into the landscapes of my soul.
Love will be my guide
Following the light
To that happy place
Where I'm just crazy enough
To believe that there are Answers for everything!
And all too soon it draws to a close
And we must seek it again, tomorrow.

Renovation of my soul

For many years nothing changed
Everything stayed the same
And I accepted it as my fate –
This is how it is meant to be –
Yes, it is Karma.

Now everything has changed
Reality has changed
And now I have a choice
To live life to the full!
The search light of truth
Shines in my soul
And somethings must change.
The rules and beliefs
I held as true,
Now seem inadequate
And these new truths
Demand an answer –
The world of possibilities
Lies before me.

All I have to do is
Admit that I was wrong,
On so many things
And embrace life
And live it.

With a shock I realise
That what I thought
Was unchangeable
Is actually malleable and fluid!

The connection
Thoughts – energy – body
Spiritual– eternity – God.
I must fly!

Ian Hibburt

Thoughts of a Monk

We are all here to learn
Said the Abbot.

And what did I learn
In the confines of
This monastery?

I learnt self-discipline
And going without –
I learnt self-sacrifice
And surrender,
I learnt to be self-contained
Needing no-one else.

I learnt the disappointment
Of Praying to a God who
Is un-moved by your entreaties

I also learnt to find joy
In the smallest things
A flower growing in a crack of the wall
A bird flying high
Against the bluest sky
Singing its song of love

And I learnt patience and
Contentment in routine
The pleasure of growing things and
Working in the gardens.

I also learnt to read the Holy Books
And sing the hymns of praise.

The Monk climbed the monastery
Bell tower and looked out
To the far horizons
Just then two Eagles
Flew over gracefully
Riding the winds
Eventually disappearing from sight
"Oh that I could fly away,
Strong and free like those Eagles
But I am imprisoned behind these
Walls of lies and rules.
One day I will break free"
The Monk thought

And he did.

Ian Hibburt

In Between

I'm not awake
I'm not asleep
I'm in between
In that place
Where ideas come and go
And tell you what you know.

I'm not hungry
I'm not full
I'm in between – content.

I'm not Happy
I'm not Sad
I'm good-content.

I'm not Rich
I'm not Poor
I have enough
Not wanting more.

I'm not high
I'm not low
In between,
In the flow.

I'm not lost
I'm not found
I'm just looking around.

In between is
Where I am
Not left or right
Hot or cold
Not one extreme
Or the other.

I'm not black or white
I have a third choice
That's in between
Both extremes.

Judgement was the thing
Right or wrong
Nothing else –
I divided my life into
Good or bad
Splitting life into two halves
With no remainder
Sharp and clean
Black or white –
But there's a world
Of many greys
Many ways besides
Right and wrong.

Ian Hibburt

So now my world
Is full of possibilities,
Opportunities,
So I'm suspending judgement
I'm exploring the
Vast world, of in between.

Some see life in black and white
Or view it through the Prism
Of judgement,
White light divided
Into seven colours only

Differentiating the world
Into seven colours is useful
But it is not all of the truth –
It is arbitrary and ignores
The millions of colours
In between.

Chapter 4

LOVE

A Rose in a Cemetery

Among the tall trees
Rows of ancient tombstones
Are on parade
Gently the wind breathes
Memories of times gone by.
Mary Manson – died in childbirth
James Brown 13yrs 9mths drowned
These lives of the old pioneers
So optimistic
And so tragic.
My Love and I contemplate
While walking by
I pick a Rose the colour of flesh
From beside a grave.
The dead will not object
They have all moved on
But this Rose, like our Love
Will give its beauty,
Then will die, a reminder
Of loves gone by.

She Cries

I came upon an Angel in a graveyard
My Angel "why do you cry"?
Tears from your eyes
And from your heart
What can it be?
That makes you so sad
Surely it must be bad

She looked up at me and said,
"I cry for the dead, those who died alone
And thought their life was in vain"

But surely, I said, they must have had
Friends or lovers to comfort them –
"No" she said. "loneliness is crushing –
An unbearable pain in the heart"
What can I do? I asked.
For these it is too late.
But as you go through life
Look out for that lonely soul
And give them a smile and say hello –
Make friendship your way of healing
The lonely in this world.

Alright I said, and if I can,
There will be one less lonely soul
You won't have to cry for.

Love Saved Me

Love saved me,
Love of a woman
Love opened my eyes
To the truth.
In finding you,
I found myself
Oh what a journey
It has been.
My beliefs have been challenged
And many have crumbled
In the light of pure love.
Love has healed my soul
Love has given me
Hope and joy again.

Our Love

Everything has changed since we fell in Love
The world is a brighter place, smiles upon our faces
Living in the joy of loving each other
To Love and be Loved in return
Is the greatest gift you could ever earn.
She gives to me the Love I need
And I Love her with all my soul.
To be entwined in the energy of pure Love
Is to become one with each other and with God
Completeness fills my soul
And we are living on the edge of eternity.
Love is eternal.

Sleep My Angel

Lying there, relaxed and at peace
Sleep my Angel
You are so beautiful
Spending your life Loving others
Now, you can rest
You are safe in my arms
Journeying in your dreams to those
Far lands of goodness and light
Filling your heart with Joy and Love.
We are in that miraculous place
Where anything is possible
And reality can be bent
To serve a higher purpose
So sleep my Angel
Dream on
Dream happiness
Dream Love –
Sleep my Angel

Last flight to Venus

The last flight to Venus is leaving
This is the last chance to find Love
Last chance to change your life,
Yes it will cost you
And you must leave it all behind.
No more playing it safe
No more comfort zone
No more boredom
And slow death.
No going back
Once we leave that's it!
And Oh the glory of deep space
The mysteries of light and power
Open your mind to the impossible
That you are seeing right here.
We are headed to the planet of Love
Out here where miracles are normal
And the impossible is unknown.
Who wants to leave their comfort zone?
I did and have never regretted that decision.

Our Bridge

Cling to me
Face our fears together
Hand in hand,
Arm in arm,
Over the Bridge
From the old to the new.
Across the river of sorrow
Our heart's warm glow guides us
Across the river of sadness
To the sunshine of our Love
Standing in our promised land
That Happy feeling
Bubbles up within
Ecstasy, Bliss and Happiness
It has begun ...

I Love You When ...

I love you when
You are lying there asleep,
I love you when
The sun kisses your cheek
I love you when
You smile with your eyes
Deep into my soul.
I love you with each
Intimate caress
I love you when you kiss me
And the whole world turns.
Giving in to the tenderness
And primal power
Of our tight embrace.

Precious Thing

Love is the rain that falls
As tears on to dry land.
Love is the Sun that shines
After the darkest night
To warm our hearts
Love is the wind that
Breathes within us.
When you have found Love –
It is everywhere
But when you lose Love
You will search in vain
To find it anywhere
So your Love is a precious thing
Never let it go.

May the Angels

May the Angels walk with you
Angels of Mercy, Love and Power,
To guide you on your way
Keep seeking the beauty in this world.
Follow the light and you will be
Blessed in all that you do.

Chapter 5
GREEN NATURE

My Day has Begun

The morning Sun sparkled –
Sky as clear as pale Lapis Lazuli

Sulphur Crested Cockatoos screeched
As they flew in formation
Two Crows talked quietly under a tree

Flocks of Galahs flew by
In a hurry to be somewhere
New summer growth shines,
Emerald green.

What a beautiful morning,
But as I turn into Hamilton Street

The vicious Kilmore Wind assails me
Blowing up from the southern ocean
Born in the ice and snow of Antarctica
It chills me, but it is clean and cold.
My day has begun.

Mid Winter

The leaves are gone
And the trees are bare,
Naked against a grey sky.

A black Crow roosts on a branch
Silently cursing the cold.

This is mid winter
The nadir of nature
The pause before we begin
Inching towards spring.

But, the wild Plum is in blossom
Declaring its faith
In the coming spring

We must patiently await
The return of spring
When energy returns
And life speeds up again.

Morning

Standing here on the edge
Of the Earth
With the morning sun
In my eyes
Crisp cool winter air
In my lungs
The sparkle of sunlight
Flashing through dew drops
And I feel alive
invigorated, a tingle, oneness –
Communion
With creation and the creator.
Ah ... yes.

Mountain Brumbies

Quietly the horses
Appeared from the scrub
Making their way down
To the stream,
Nervously drinking the refreshing water
Eyes and ears alert
Ready to run at the first sign
Of trouble.
These are the mountain brumbies
Born wild and free
Un-tamed!
Proud and strong
This is where they belong.

The Tides

Imperceptibly it changes
The outward flow stops
And for a time nothing moves.
Then the inward flow begins
And salty water fills the bay.

The oceans love affair with the
Moon ebbs and flows
Like the ocean breathing
It creates its own rhythm
In measured progression.

And all those creatures great and small
Dance in time to the rhythm of the tides
And the wise ones live in tune
With the seasons and pulse
Of the earth.

Stars are shining

Stars are shining
Out in the bright void of space.

The eternals are singing
The songs of creation
This is the infinite universe
Forever unfolding outwards

The Earth contains the
Fingerprints of design
And our lives contain
The signature of the creator,
But,
The Earth is wrapped in the stress
Of our own making
Consuming itself in
Man made dramas.

The Crows

Ten of them there were
Sitting on the power lines
All facing my direction.

That's unusual I thought
Two or three that's normal
But ten crows assembled together,
It seems so formal.
What's the meaning of this meeting?

Some people are scared of Crows
Related to Ravens and Rooks
Harbingers of death they say
But Australian Crows are different.

They are intelligent and skilful birds
The Noongar people of WA say:
They are the souls of important people
Returned to earth as Crows.

To have them here is an honour
Why are you here?
Respect passes between us,
Each from different worlds
But connected in an ethereal way

They have said what they came to say
And now they fly away,
All except my three locals.

Ian Hibburt

Reflections on a River

So still, so quiet,
Tranquillity and peace

Here my mind is stilled
And my soul is at rest
Far away from the rushing city
And it's pressure

Here I can listen to
The sounds of nature,
Kookaburras laughing
In the distance,
Frogs sing their love songs.
Clouds slide by – above
Sunlight filters through the trees
Energising the landscape.

Yes, I'm glad I stopped
And broke my journey here.

Southern Ocean

With a measured thwump ... thwump
Waves smash against the cliffs
The sound of the ocean breathing.

The blue horizon stretches forever
Blue water against blue sky
White foam against sandstone cliffs
Standing here; being part of this.

Away from the rush of city life
I settle into the rhythm of nature
I'm developing an affinity
To the slow beat of the seasons
And the journeying of the stars
Across their indigo skies.

Ian Hibburt

The Beach on the Edge of the World

Children playing in the sand
Happy shouts above the roar
Of the waves.
Seagulls cry as the sun sinks
Into the western sea
Driftwood fires burn
As the fishermen return
Cooking dinner on the coals
Twilight approaches quietly
And the world slumbers
In the fading light
Starlight twinkles in the sky
And a sickle moon rides delicately
In the scarlet waves.
Such peace and happiness
Dwells here, at the beach
On the edge of the world.

Pukekura Park

Grandparents, parents and children –
We are all at the park today
Children laughing, playing
In the spring sunshine.
Ducks are swimming on the lake
Rushing in to catch the bread we throw
Feeding the Ducks, it's why we come here
To Pukekura Park –
Or do we come here to be a family
Doing family things together?

Ian Hibburt

Family Beach Time

Playing in the sand
Sea gulls cry, crowding the sky
Swimming in the surf
Salty freshness on our skin,
Lying in the sun to get warm again
Days at the beach
Are my best memories
Sitting around the fire at night
Reading stories to our children
Then off to bed to dream
Of summer days.

The Pelicans Have Gone

Such a noble bird, graceful in flight.
At ease on the water, but awkward on the land
All through the summer and into the autumn
They were to be seen fishing in the lakes
Flying the skies of blue

Cold and grey winter skies are now all I see
And my friends the Pelicans are gone.
Smart birds they are, probably in Queensland by now
Sitting in the sun on some sandy beach
Having had their fill of their favourite fish
Yes, you are smarter than me
Summer down south and winter up north
You've got it right my friends
And I'll see you again when the skies are blue
And the warm sun shines again.

The Forest Chapel

Down
the secret track
Visible only to those
Who know of its existence
Winding through the bush
And among the Giant Redwoods
Is the pathway in the forest
The air is charged with Green Energy
And the Earth beneath my feet
Is a carpet of growing things
And massive trees make a cathedral
Branches
Arching
Overhead
Protecting
A glade
Of Green Energy

Chapter 6

TRUTH & CHANGE

A tear silently falls

Seeking truth will make me
Regret the truths that I find.
There's no denying this;
Yes, I was wrong
Things I learnt and was taught
Were only half-right
And would never give
Their promised fulfilment.
Like everyone else I assumed
I was at fault, not working hard enough
No. I was lied to –
And now that I know this,
I regret the lost opportunities for
Love and Happiness.

No blame, no grief, just
The cold hard truth.
But it will cleanse my mind
Of the wrong thoughts and lies
To replace them with real truth.
No need to pretend anymore
No fantasy to feed and support.
Don't hook me into your dramas,
Because I won't help you!
Don't seek my approval constantly –
If you do well, that is enough!
I have my own life to live
My own pathway to follow –
You are welcome to follow
In my footsteps, if you wish,
But it will always be an individual quest
We are responsible for ourselves.

Truth

So this is it,
This is the beginning
Or is it the end?

The end of the lies
The beginning of the truth

The truth lies hidden
Like a fallen tombstone
In the graveyard of lost dreams

Covered with dead things
Autumn leaves, dirt and detritus
Hidden from sight
The real story never told.

Till we all believed it was just
A fairytale from days gone by
The story now twisted beyond recognition
But what is this? People come,
Looking for the truth
Clearing away the lies and deception
Here it is – the Truth,
Carved in stone – unchanging.

Finally the truth is heard,
And the wrongs righted
The shadows flee from
The light of the truth
And we are indeed FREE.

Ian Hibburt

Gates of Paradise

And how do we return
To the age of innocence?
How do we silence the
Voice that condemns us?
Are we doomed to wander the earth
In search of our lost innocence?
Do we seek the impossible dream?
We have been led astray
And been sold lies and half truths
If we are all sinners
And Jesus died to free us
Why is nobody free?
Why do we have to wait
Till we die then go to heaven?
Are we doomed to wander
Outside the Gates of Paradise?
One bad decision and
Mankind is condemned.
We did not know we were bad
Until someone told us.
Aw shit! This is complicated.

Yes, there are bad people
Very bad people and
I suppose at some point
They chose the dark side
And gave themselves over
To their evil desires –
And yet others don't.
They lead a life
Trying to do the right thing
So it seems to go in two stages
Born innocent,
Told that they are sinners and
What is right and wrong
Then a choice is made
Follow God or follow the Devil.
But here's the problem –
Those who follow God
Cannot go back to Paradise
Because they "know" that
They are sinners.
What if the serpent lied to them?
And we know he was a liar
And still is –

We believed his lies
When we were innocent children
So to regain Paradise
We stop believing the lies
And silence the voice of the serpent
And listen to our original
Authentic, innocent self
Who still believes in a good God
Who made us sinless.
So when we approach the Gates
Of Paradise and see the Angel
With the flaming sword which
Turns in all directions,
The Angel will say
"You cannot enter – you have sinned"
Then I say "I don't believe I am a sinner,
That is a lie. I believe God made me sinless"
The Angel then says "Enter".

The New Normal

So this is the new normal
Life is changing and resetting
To the new normal.
Living your dreams is now
Possible – even essential

Before we were lost in the woods
Seeking a way out.
Surrounded on every side
By problems,
Not knowing the way home.

Then we met a guide
Who led us out.
He bade us farewell
At the forest's edge
"Now you are free,
Free to live your dreams!"

Ian Hibburt

The Halls of Knowledge?

Are not your bookcases filled with
All manner of books?
Yes, they are.
Does not your pantry
Contain the makings
Of fabulous meals?
Is not your bed
An altar of Love
Where pleasure and joy
Are revered?
Do not your rooms contain
Treasures of beauty and art?
And all those arts and craft
Resources are just waiting to be used.

Yes I have been blind
To the reality that has
Been hiding in plain sight.

Look again the Angel said,
What you need, you already have.
Change your perception
Change your reality.

There is no end
To wanting more
The more you feed avarice
The bigger it becomes.

So be happy with where you are,
What you have –
The family you are in
The Love you have
Appreciate it, build it
Own it.

Ian Hibburt

The beauty of Healing

I'm so thankful to those healers out there
Who gently heal our hearts, minds and bodies
I was broken, confused and sick
And I discovered the healers
And they guided me to find the way
To full health and happiness.

There is a place of light, love and joy
Where you can go,
Leave all negativity, judgement and criticism
At the gate, and walk right in.

There surrender yourself to the kind
And gentle ministrations of the healers
These healers are God's friends,
Spiritual beings living in a world
Just above us humans
Where we can go
When the path we know.

Nothing is impossible with these guys
Your past painful memories
Can be desensitised –
Yes, that painful thing happened
But it does not hurt now
And I can see this good thing
Came out of it.

Your heart broken?
It can be fixed.
Trust the healers to guide you
To the people you need.

Physical healing is easy
When your heart and mind is strong,
Answers and solutions
Will become obvious.
So thank you to the healers –
Givers of life, love and joy.
Once you've met them
Your lives will never be the same

Small Lives

Some people live small lives
Being cautious, following the rules.
Doing what they're told.
Slowly growing old.
Confident in the safeness of their
Uneventful life.
As their life slowly closes in.

The farm, hundreds of acres.
Then the home in town
With large gardens,
Then the town house
With the tiny back garden,
Then the single room in the nursing home
And finally the coffin.
So predictable.
What of all those missed opportunities –
What of those unused abilities?
Died on the vine.

What of the Beauty and Joy you ignored
In your pursuit of safety?

And it is gone –
You've missed it.
Last flight to Venus
You've been left behind.
In your comfort zone.

Oh yes I know the Logic;
"You can't fail if you don't try!"
But, you fail to try!

Step out of your comfort zone
Risk something and win a bit of Joy
And happiness.
Oh Fuck … it's like trying to explain flying to turkeys!
They just don't get it.
Is it possible for turkeys
To transform into eagles?
I guess so, I was a turkey, once.

Says the Brown Owl

I am small, but I know
The secrets of the heart.
And I can see in the darkness –
Night vision.

I have the ability to perceive
What is hidden from normal sight
And I have drawn back the veil of darkness
That was preventing you seeing the truth.

"Better something than nothing" you said
Tolerate the lie so that the relationship
Can continue, and that works for a while.
But, the lie continues to grow unchecked
Until, like my friend the Elephant,
It fills the room!

And there it is the nasty truth!
Once you see it,
You can't un-see it.
And I thank you for
Showing me the truth.

It is a truth that demands action,
Demands an answer.
Embrace the lie and be taken over
By deception and pretence –
This way lies madness!

Or, discard this aberration
Of what was once true,
Walk away and keep your
Integrity and sanity.

Thank you Brown Owl for
Laying this out so clearly
You are a true friend.

White Eagle Returns

"We are all given knowledge
To use and get understanding"

We all have a choice between
The truth and the lie –

The truth is hard, like a diamond,
And requires purity and courage
To face our faults.

The lie is soft, like a bed,
Easy, and encourages us to blame others
For our faults.

The truth will make you strong,
Pure and true.

The lie will make you weak,
Corrupt and dishonest.

Choose one way to follow,
They are both mutually exclusive.
Light and darkness cannot dwell
In the same house together

The Elephant Again

It's getting crowded in here
The Elephant looks at me,
Ian, he says, what's happening?
Just the usual; three o'clock
In the morning and I can't sleep.
Yes, a lot has happened
Since we last talked.
Your poems are in a book
For all to read
If it's inspiration that they need.

Yes, I remembered my dreams
And I have gone back to
The age of innocence
And I am reminded to
Deeply experience emotions
The let them go –

And now what do you say?
FIGHT! – FIGHT for what you know is right
Set your goals and make
Them come true.

Be strong like me – nothing stops me
If I want to go in a certain direction
I just push through.

Maybe you need to make room
In your life for new things,
Expand your reality
Push back the walls!

Once you were a maze runner
Then you tired of that
And created an exit door
Now you are a bit confined
By lack of skills and need
A road map to get to your destination.
and road blocks appear.
But now, do what I do,
Push through these roadblocks
Push through those walls.
Magic Elephant
Mover of obstacles

Thank you Jumbo, you've given me
A lot to think about and do.

Second Destiny

So that didn't work out.
That's interesting, did you learn anything?
Well, yes, it's just a pity that it's taken so long
For me to discover the ugly truth that I've been used,
Taken for a sucker, used and fed a lie,
Gullible me ... Nice one guys!
No more! This stops! This ends now!
The game is ended.

Walking away now.
Walking away now.
Things to do for me
Time to find my second destiny
Time for me to complete my task.
Irresistible force to create new pathways
For mankind to walk.
Positive life affirming beliefs
A space for Love, Joy and Harmony to grow,
It is our destiny to choose, or reject.
Choose the good and let it grow.

Night Steed

My night steed, the colour of shadows
Is waiting for me to ride into
Indigo night skies
To follow the dreams of my heart
Across the landscape
On the wings of my soul
Fantastic lands of "other" worlds
Are waiting for me to explore
There I meet the wise ones
To commune and share
Their eternal wisdom

I awake from my dreams
With a deep knowing
That there is more to this life
Than I will ever know.

www.ingramcontent.com/pod-product-compliance
Lightning Source LLC
Chambersburg PA
CBHW040416100526
44588CB00022B/2847